PLANT
DEFENSES

PLANTS THAT HIDE

DEVI PURI

PowerKiDS press

New York

Published in 2017 by The Rosen Publishing Group, Inc.
29 East 21st Street, New York, NY 10010

First Edition

Editor: Sarah Machajewski
Book Design: Reann Nye

Photo Credits: Cover Martin Harvey/Photolibrary/Getty Images; p. 4 Pan Xunbin/ Shutterstock.com; p. 5 kurt_G/Shutterstock.com; p. 6 Petlia Roman/Shutterstock.com; p. 7 Steve Brigman/Shutterstock.com; p. 8 Julien_N/Shutterstock.com; p. 9 Mike Kemp Images/The Image Bank/Getty Images; p. 10 kowit sitthi/Shutterstock.com; p. 11 Michael Richardson/Shutterstock.com; p. 12 Bildagentur Zoonar GmbH/ Shutterstock.com; p. 13 Olga_Anourina/Shutterstock.com; p. 14 https://commons. wikimedia.org/wiki/File:Monotropsis_odorata.jpg; p. 15 Gregory A. Pozhvanov/ Shutterstock.com; p. 16 Four Oaks/Shutterstock.com; p. 17 FotoRequest/ Shutterstock.com; p. 18 bravo1954/E+/Getty Images; p. 19 (top) Westend61/ Getty Images; p. 19 (bottom) Kira_Yan/Shutterstock.com; p. 20 janews/ Shutterstock.com; p. 21 https://commons.wikimedia.org/wiki/File:Caladium_ white1.JPG; p. 22 Vysokova Ekaterina/Shutterstock.com.

Cataloging-in-Publication Data

Names: Puri, Devi.
Title: Plants that hide / Devi Puri.
Description: New York : PowerKids Press, 2017. | Series: Plant defenses | Includes index.
Identifiers: ISBN 9781499421439 (pbk.) | ISBN 9781499421453 (library bound) | ISBN 9781499421446 (6 pack)
Subjects: LCSH: Plants–Adaptation–Juvenile literature. | Plants–Juvenile literature.
Classification: LCC QK912.P87 2017 | DDC 581.4–dc23

Manufactured in the United States of America

CPSIA Compliance Information: Batch #BS16PK: For Further Information contact Rosen Publishing, New York, New York at 1-800-237-9932

CONTENTS

DON'T RUN!............4

PLAYING DEFENSE.......6

ADAPTING TO
     SURVIVE..............10

LIVING STONES........12

DEAD-ON LOOKS........14

SECRET SEEDS.........16

WHAT'S THAT WEED?..18

SO SICK!..............20

SKILLFUL SURVIVORS..22

GLOSSARY.............23

INDEX................24

WEBSITES.............24

DON'T RUN!

What would you do if you wanted to get away from danger? You'd probably run—fast! Plants face danger, too, but they're firmly planted in the ground. They can't exactly run away. For some plants, the best way to stay safe is to hide.

Plants that hide are found all over the world. They have different ways of **concealing** themselves. Some plants hide by changing color, looking sick, or changing to look like another plant! Some like to hide by looking like nonliving objects in their **environment**. Let's explore some of the plant world's coolest defenses.

Plants aren't the only creatures that hide to stay safe. This spider and walking stick (left) are experts at blending in with their surroundings!

PLAYING DEFENSE

Imagine if you had to stay in one place your whole life. No matter what kinds of animals, bugs, people, or weather you faced, you'd have to stay put. Instead of leaving, you'd have to figure out how to survive these threats, or dangers. That's the life of a plant— and that's where defense comes in.

A defense is an organism's way of protecting itself. Some plants defend themselves with thorns, spikes, and spines. Predators know not to come near these scary-looking plants. Others may give off a bad smell or appear to look dead. Some can kill you with poison!

PLANT POINTER
Sometimes we can't clearly see a plant's defense, even though it's there. Never touch or taste a plant you're unfamiliar with.

Poison ivy can give you a rash that will make sure you never go near the plant again! That's a good defense.

Camouflage is another plant defense. This is when a plant **disguises** itself to blend in with its surroundings. It's the perfect way to hide! If predators can't see a plant, they can't eat it.

Another kind of defense is called mimicry. Mimicry is when a plant makes itself look like another plant or animal. A predator might pass by a plant if it thinks it's something else.

What's the difference between camouflage and mimicry? Think of it this way: with camouflage, plants don't want to be noticed at all. With mimicry, plants are noticed, but not for what they really are. They're hiding in plain sight!

PLANT POINTER

Plants in the wild are commonly shades of brown and green. Camouflage clothing is made to blend in with these colors.

You may have heard of camouflage clothing. People wear it when they want to blend in with nature. This is helpful for hiding in the woods!

ADAPTING TO SURVIVE

Plant defenses of all kinds are good examples of adaptations. An adaptation is a change an organism makes in order to survive in its environment.

Adaptations take a very long time to form. Camouflage may have started in plants living long ago. Plants that blended in better with their environment survived longer than ones that stood out. The surviving plants then passed this trait on to new plants. These plants also survived and passed on the trait. Over time, these plants that hide showed that blending in was the best way for them to stay safe.

PLANT POINTER

Camouflage is a good way to survive, but the opposite works, too. Brightly colored flowers draw in **pollinators** that help make new plants.

The goal of every **species** is to survive to the next **generation**. Adaptations make this possible, even in the most challenging places.

LIVING STONES

In 1811, a scientist named William John Burchell was in South Africa when he picked up what he thought was a small stone. It wasn't! It was a plant. Burchell later wrote that its color and overall look greatly **resembled** the stones sitting nearby.

What Burchell discovered was a type of *Lithops*, or living stone plant. They're sometimes called pebble plants. *Lithops* grow in the hot, dry deserts of South Africa. Their thick, rounded leaves store water, which desert animals would love to find. However, *Lithops* hide by looking like stones! Their gray, brown, and cream-colored leaves don't seem like a good source of water to even the thirstiest predators.

PLANT POINTER
Lithops leaves are often covered with tiny dots, stripes, or other markings.

A *Lithops* plant's color and shape help it hide among stones.

DEAD-ON LOOKS

Plants make their own food using sunlight, **carbon dioxide**, water, and minerals. One of the materials that helps them do this makes them green. *Monotropsis odorata* is a wild flower with pink, purple, or yellow flowers and a purple stem. This plant doesn't go through the process that would make it green.

Monotropsis odorata gets everything it needs to live from **fungi** living on its roots. Because it isn't green, it can blend in better with its surroundings. It's able to hide from predators by looking like dead plant matter. When predators see the *Monotropsis odorata*, they can't tell that it's actually a healthy, living plant.

PLANT POINTER

Even though it's a master of disguise, *Monotropsis odorata* still needs helpful pollinators to visit it. It releases a strong, sweet smell to **attract** them.

MONOTROPSIS ODORATA

LATHRAEA SQUAMARIA

Would you notice these purple flowers among the brown plant matter, or does the plant hide itself well?

SECRET SEEDS

Plants have to hide their seeds from predators, too. Seeds are a tasty meal for many kinds of creatures—especially birds. Scientists think birds are more likely to eat the seeds that stand out the most in their environment. It's easier to spot a yellow or red seed in soil than a brown one.

Some plants change the color of their seeds so they can hide in their **native soil**. For example, pine seeds may be many colors so they blend in with ash and soil in their environment. A plant called the Chilean bird's-foot trefoil produces camouflaged seeds to match the soil, too.

PLANT POINTER
If seeds are eaten, they can't grow into new plants. Hiding in soil is a great defense!

Studies have shown that predators are more likely to eat seeds that stand out in their environment.

WHAT'S THAT WEED?

Farmers remove weeds that **invade** their crops. It's usually easy to tell what's the crop and what's the weed. But what if the weed disguises itself to look like the crop? Farmers don't know which plant to pull, and both get to survive. That's the case with rye.

Rye is a grass that looks a lot like wheat. Today, we use its seeds as a grain, but it actually began as a weed. Since it looks so similar to wheat, farmers had a hard time spotting it in their fields. The overlooked rye lived and made new plants. Sometimes, hiding is the best way to survive.

PLANT POINTER

Rye actually grows better in some environments than wheat. Once farmers discovered this, they started growing it on purpose.

Rye is a great example of a plant that used mimicry to hide. Can you tell which of these crops is rye and which is wheat?

SO SICK!

In the forests of Ecuador, moths lay their eggs on a plant called *Caladium steudneriifolium*. When the eggs hatch, the young caterpillars eat the plant's leaves, leaving trails of damage behind them. Caterpillars could keep hurting the plant— unless it fakes being sick.

Scientists believe this plant changes the color of some of its leaves to look like it's already been eaten. Their markings look like white trails normally left by caterpillars. When moths see the sick-looking plant, they're less likely to lay eggs on it. Hiding behind its "sickness," *Caladium steudneriifolium* lives to see another day.

PLANT POINTER

Some *Caladium* plants can be grown as house plants. They don't hide like the *Caladium steudneriifolium*, but their coloring is similar.

The white markings on this leaf make it look sickly. Hopefully predators will think so, too!

SKILLFUL SURVIVORS

The plants you've learned about are very different, but they have something special in common—their ability to hide. This special adaptation has allowed plants to survive many kinds of threats. Some, like the living stone plant, hide to keep animals from eating them. Others, such as rye, hide to keep people from killing them.

A defense is successful if it keeps the plant alive. Hiding means plants live long enough to create seeds, which create new plants. These masters of disguise continue to live among us, even if we can't spot them. What else could be hiding out there?

GLOSSARY

attract: To draw nearer.

carbon dioxide: A gas in the air that plants use to make food.

conceal: To hide.

disguise: To make something not look like itself by changing its appearance.

environment: The natural surroundings of a person, plant, or animal.

fungus: A living thing that is somewhat like a plant, but doesn't make its own food or have leaves or a green color. Fungi include molds and mushrooms.

generation: All the plants that started growing about the same time.

invade: To spread into an area where something else is.

native soil: The unaltered soil found in an area where a plant naturally grows.

organism: An individual plant or animal.

pollinator: Something that carries pollen from one flower to another to make new plants.

resemble: To look or seem like something else.

species: A group of living organisms that have similar traits.

INDEX

B
birds, 16
Burchell, William John, 12

C
Caladium steudneriifolium, 20
camouflage, 8, 9, 10, 16
carbon dioxide, 14
caterpillars, 20
Chilean bird's-foot trefoil, 16

D
desert, 12

E
Ecuador, 20
environment, 4, 10, 16, 17, 18

L
Lithops (living stone plant), 12, 13, 22

M
mimicry, 8, 19
Monotropsis odorata, 14
moths, 20

P
pine, 16
poison ivy, 7
pollinator, 10, 14
predators, 6, 8, 12, 14, 16, 17, 21

R
rye, 18, 19, 22

S
seeds, 16, 17, 18, 22
South Africa, 12
species, 11

W
weed, 18
wheat, 18, 19

WEBSITES

Due to the changing nature of Internet links, PowerKids Press has developed an online list of websites related to the subject of this book. This site is updated regularly. Please use this link to access the list: www.powerkidslinks.com/plantd/hide